VAK Self-Audit

Visual, Auditory, and Kinesthetic
Communication and Learning Styles

Exploring patterns of how you interact and learn

Brian Everard Walsh PhD Mnlp

PUBLISHING HOUSE

VAK Self-Audit
Visual, Auditory, and Kinesthetic Communication and Learning Styles

Copyright © 2011 Walsh Seminars Publishing House

Neurolinguistic Programming (NLP) language is widely used. Phrases or full sentences may duplicate or resemble material found elsewhere. Some passages are impossible to cite since the original sources are not known. Apologies to any and all unidentified sources.

Library and Archives Canada Cataloguing in Publication

Walsh, Brian Everard, 1947-
    VAK self-audit : visual, auditory, and kinesthetic communication and learning styles : exploring patterns of how you interact and learn / Brian E. Walsh.

ISBN 978-0-9866655-5-4

    1. Learning. 2. Interpersonal communication. 3. Self-perception.
I. Title.

LB1060.W24 2011   370.15'23   C2011-902331-8

Editors: Astrid Whiting and Ron Willard
Thanks also to Anna Lisa Bond, Gregg Turner, Michael Losier, and Roger Ellerton
Illustrations by iStockphoto   Author photo by Frances Litman Photography Inc.

Also available as an eBook ISBN 978-0-9866655-1-6

More paperbacks by this same author

- Unleashing Your Brilliance ISBN 9780973841510
- Emergency Responder Communication Skills Handbook ISBN 9780986665509
- BrainWidth ISBN 978-0-9866655-3-0

Walsh Seminars Ltd.
Box 963, Victoria BC V8W 2R9 Canada

MESSAGE SENT ≠ MESSAGE RECEIVED

Confusion and misunderstandings happen for many reasons

People communicate, both verbally and nonverbally, in a diversity of styles. It's almost as if they are speaking different languages to each other.

Knowing how these styles differ can help you put your ideas across more clearly, and give your point of view greater acceptance. As well, you'll have a better handle on the messages people are sending and saying to you.

It just makes sense to learn and use these skills.

Once you understand the different profiles, you can

- get your point across in a way that people will understand
- establish rapport quickly to facilitate smother interactions
- absorb information with greater ease and comprehension
- enhance your leadership skills and accelerate your career

There are many communication models.

This particular one, from the field of *Neurolinguistic Programming* (NLP), is commonly known as VAK (*Visual, Auditory, and Kinesthetic*).

This book includes a fourth profile. In NLP terms, it is known as *Auditory Digital* (Ad). In this text, to better describe what's happening, I call it *Internal Dialogue* (Id). That also avoids confusion with ADD, a term not yet known when NLP was originally developed.

The full **VAK-Id model** is quite detailed, so in this book I will provide just a brief overview.

As we begin to explore VAK-Id, remember that, as with other models, all of us possess varying mixtures of all profiles.

As with most abilities, these communication skills will quickly improve with practice. To start the process, begin using these concepts in your everyday communication at work and at home. In time, your improved capabilities and skills will become second nature.

To better understand this communications model, do these three steps.
1. *Learn the characteristics of the four profiles*
2. *Do the short review exercise*
3. *Take the Self-Audit*

NLP could be the most important synthesis of knowledge about human communication to emerge since the explosion of humanistic psychology in the sixties.

Science Digest

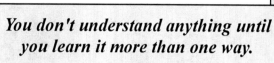

> *You don't understand anything until you learn it more than one way.*
> Marvin Minsky

The overview of each of the four profiles found in the next few pages will give you the grounding required for a solid understanding of this communication model.

Each consists of three components:

1. Characteristics
2. Words and phrases used by this style
3. Best practices for learning

Visual

1. Characteristics

These Communicators . . .
- must see to learn
- breathe high in the chest
- gesture up with their hand
- have a higher-pitched voice
- are neat and orderly
- lift up their head
- look up when talking
- are organized and observant
- prefer to read rather than be read to
- are easily distracted by visual stimuli
- are not usually distracted by noise
- stand erect shoulders straight across
- stand back so as to "take it all in"
- remember what they see, rather than hear
- recall faces better than names
- prefer one-on-one interactions
- may have difficulty with verbal instructions

> *Do you know the difference between education and experience?*
> *Education is when you read the fine print; experience is what you get when you don't.*
> Pete Seeger

2. Words & Phrases They Use

- I see what you mean
- Looking ahead
- You'll look back at this and laugh
- The future looks bright
- It appears to me
- This will shed some light on the matter
- Taking a dim view
- Sight for sore eyes
- Mind's eye
- It colors his view of life
- I am looking closely at the idea
- I have a hazy notion
- Beyond a shadow of a doubt
- Well that's your point of view
- Watch what she says now
- Explain it again, it isn't clear to me yet
- I can imagine what you mean
- We must focus on this issue
- That's brilliant
- Picture this
- That's my perspective

3. Best Practices for Learning

Color-code your notes
Use pictures and diagrams
Use charts for outlines and note-taking
Remember what you <u>see</u>, rather than hear
Spelling is improved by visualizing words
Memorize using pictures & Mind Maps

Auditory

1. Characteristics

These Communicators

- are great orators
- speak clearly
- are easily distracted by noise
- are talkative, love their own voice
- tilt their head as if on the phone
- hold their shoulders back
- have rhythmic breathing - sigh
- learn by listening
- drum their fingers or tap their toes
- move eyes side-to-side (not up or down)
- have difficulty with written directions
- talk to themselves while thinking
- remember conversations well

---

*Looking back, you realize that everything
would have explained itself
if you had only stopped interrupting.*
Robert Brault

Never miss a good chance to shut up.
Will Rogers

2. Words & Phrases They Use

- Loud & clear
- It rings a bell
- In a manner of speaking
- Unheard of
- I love the accent in your decor
- Turn a deaf ear
- That's all Greek to me
- He is within earshot
- On the same wavelength
- Music to my ears
- The squeaky wheel...
- Living in harmony
- He's calling the tune
- Tell me
- A lot of babbling
- Sounds good to me
- Rings true
- End with a bang
- Please amplify on that
- On another note
- Voiced an opinion

3. Best Practices for Learning

Record information & play back
Participate in discussions
Have someone read to you
Practice by asking questions
Listen to Baroque music
Read aloud

Kinesthetic

1. Characteristics

These Communicators

- have gut feelings
- breathe low and deep in the abdomen
- have a low pitch voice and slower tone
- speak slowly and use action words
- can't sit still for long periods (antsy)
- stand close when talking
- are well coordinated - have athletic abilities
- gesture down by their middle or stomach
- point to their heart
- look down
- want to act things out
- touch people to get their attention
- touch people when greeting or leaving
- are often huggers
- may have messy handwriting
- dress more for comfort than for looks

> *If you are seeking creative ideas,*
> *go out walking.*
>
> *Angels whisper to a man*
> *when he goes for a walk.*
>
> Raymond Inmon

2. Words & Phrases They Use

- Got a handle on
- Get a grip
- Get a hold of yourself
- Hang in there
- Do you feel left out
- That was hard
- Thick-skinned
- Don't be so touchy
- Out of touch
- Make contact
- Tap into our resources
- Hand in hand
- I can grasp that idea
- Show me what you mean
- Turn the business around
- Hold on a second
- I will get in touch with you
- Scratch the surface
- I can't put my finger on it

3. Best Practices for Learning

Take many breaks while studying
Trace letters & words

Experience and do . . .
role-play, lab work, touch

Memorize better when . . .
walking, dancing, exercising
walk and read cue cards that you've written

Internal dialogue

1. Characteristics

These Communicators . . .

- love lists
- summarize efficiently
- talk inwardly to themselves
- process internally (formulate, wonder, remember, recite)
- learn by working things out in their mind
- aren't spontaneous (have to think things through)
- thrive on concepts, systems, relationships, and models
- often believe that Id was actually a live conversation
- have a need to know if something makes sense
- are meticulous at tracking & categorizing experiences
- use facts, figures, and logic in their decision-making
- set directions and make plans as a matter of course
- can give running commentary on raw data
- can draw conclusions effectively
- have excellent recall (minds acts like a filing system)
- memorize by steps, procedures, and sequences
- must figure things out & know what makes things tick
- often take notes and will home in on the details
- are likely technically astute (expect others to be also)
- may appear dispassionate and calculating
- can join the dots where others miss the implications
- often display characteristics of VAK across the board

Nowhere am I so desperately needed as among a shipload of illogical humans.

Spock

---

2. Words & Phrases They Use

- Analyze this and get back to me
- Be sensible!
- Can you conceive this?
- Chart our progress
- Consider all the alternatives
- Decide when you get all the facts
- Describe in detail
- He needs to pay attention to ...
- How insensitive they are
- I am motivated
- I have to make sense of ...
- I know how logical this seems
- I know this system works
- I question your due diligence
- I'll sum up what we've discussed
- It stands to reason
- It's only common sense
- Let's figure out what changes are necessary
- List all the steps necessary
- No doubt
- Planning is critical
- The process for change
- There is a distinct benefit
- Think about it and then act
- Understand the process
- Yes, that makes sense

3. Best Practices for Learning
Use all the tips from VAK

Review Quiz to Test Your Knowledge

V, A, K or Id? Mark on a separate sheet of paper.
Answers to this quiz are on page 37.

Which profile does each of the following suggest?

1. are talkative - love their own voice
2. have gut feelings
3. have rhythmic breathing, sigh
4. may have difficulty with verbal instructions
5. processes situations internally before acting
6. may have difficulty with written directions
7. stand back - so as to "take it all in"
8. remember conversations well
9. can't sit still for long periods (antsy)
10. drum their fingers or tap their toes
11. touch people to get their attention
12. uses facts and logic in their decision-making
13. talk to themselves while thinking
14. are easily distracted by noise
15. enjoys concepts, systems, and links
16. point to, or put hand on, their heart
17. have a low pitch voice and slower tone
18. breathe high in the chest
19. point to their ear
20. have a higher-pitched voice, speak quickly
21. tilt their head as if on the phone
22. breathe low and deep in the abdomen
23. are good mechanically
24. speak slowly and use action words
25. learn by listening
26. are well coordinated and have athletic abilities
27. stand close when talking
28. can find meaning when others miss the point
29. are fussy about how they look to others
30. have to think things through

Perspectives, Sayings, and Thoughts

Of all the senses, sight must be the most delightful. Helen Keller

 All of us are watchers - of television, of time clocks, of traffic on the freeway - - but few are observers. Everyone is looking - - - not many are seeing. Peter M. Leschak

Who looks outside, dreams; who looks inside, awakes. C.G. Jung

---

Once a word has been allowed to escape, it cannot be recalled. Horace

It is better to keep one's mouth shut and be thought a fool than to open it and resolve all doubt. Abraham Lincoln

Don't speak unless you can improve on the silence. Spanish Proverb

---

Thoughts come clearly while one walks. Thomas Mann

 Often the hands will solve a mystery that the intellect has struggled with in vain. C. G. Jung

Tell me and I forget; show me and I remember; involve me and I understand. Anonymous

---

I paint objects as I think them, not as I see them. Pablo Picasso

Did you ever stop to think, and forget to start again? Winnie the Pooh

I think; therefore, I am "Id" Matthew Ashdown

The inability to make a decision has often been passed off as patience. Author Unknown

THE SELF-AUDIT

The following *subjective assessment* is designed to help you discover your primary communication profile.

Your unique profile simply sheds light on how you relate as a human being, and it reveals how you run your relationships. As well, it suggests how you learn and probably teach.

How to Complete the Self-Audit

Keep track of your choices on a separate sheet of paper with four columns headed: **V A K Id.**

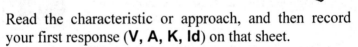

Read the characteristic or approach, and then record your first response (**V, A, K, Id**) on that sheet.

Since people play many roles in life, they often display distinct characteristics in different environments. For instance, someone at work might tend to be Visual, while in their personal life, more Kinesthetic.

To account for this, we have divided the Self-Audit into two contexts: **Work Life** and **Personal Life**.

Complete the survey twice.

1. **For Work Life, complete pages 15 thru 22 ONLY**
   For example: **If I'm angry** (*at boss, co-worker, client*), **I tend to ...**

2. **For Personal Life, complete pages 15 through 31**
   For example: **If I'm angry** (*at spouse, child, gardener*), **I tend to ...**

   - *If an answer doesn't immediately come to mind, do it later or ignore it.*
   - *If a particular attribute does not apply to you in that role, just ignore it.*
   - *Do only as many as required for you to notice your pattern.*

THE SELF-AUDIT

If I'm angry, I tend to:

V	Keep seeing in my mind what it is that has upset me
A	Raise my voice
K	Physically demonstrate my anger (thump, bang, crash) Punch walls, slam fists, or slam doors
Id	Have difficulty understanding the other side

I get along better with people who:

V	Relate to the world through the way it looks
A	Relate to the world through the way it sounds
K	Relate to the world through the way it makes them feel
Id	Think first - before they act or say something

When someone asks me to do something, it is easier to understand and to execute if:

V	It's written / illustrated / drawn in a way that I can see what to do
A	It's explained to me
K	Someone allows me to practice it first
Id	It is precise and has clarity of purpose and has sequence or order

THE SELF-AUDIT

	When I get totally motivated, the first thing that happens is:
V	I see things from a new resourceful perspective
A	I tell myself how this state is going to create new possibilities
K	I can actually feel myself getting psyched up
Id	I think of ways to complete the task

	When I spell, I verify accuracy by:
V	Looking at the word in my mind's eye to see if it looks the way that word should
A	Saying the word out loud or hearing it in my mind
K	Getting a feeling about how it's spelled
Id	Judging how logical it appears and sounds

	When anxious, the very first thing that happens is:
V	The world takes on a different appearance somehow
A	Sounds begin to bother me
K	My sense of ease begins to alter
Id	I am aware that things just don't make sense

THE SELF-AUDIT

When I have occasion to use mathematics, I verify my answer by:

V Looking at the numbers to see if they look correct

A Saying it out loud to assess the confidence in my voice

K Using my fingers to get a sense of correctness

Id Counting the numbers in my head

Having rapport with someone is:

V Seeing him or her in a wonderful and easy-to-be-with way

A Hearing the person communicate things exactly the way I would

K Feeling toward the person the way I know he or she feels toward me

Id A knowingness that we are of like minds

When I operate new equipment I generally:

V Look at the instructions so I can visualize how it works

A Listen to an explanation from someone who has used it before

K Jump right in and begin using it

Id Like to know exactly how everything works

THE SELF-AUDIT

When I dislike someone,
I get an immediate experience of dislike:

V	When I see him or her approach
A	When he or she begins talking to me
K	When I sense him or her nearby
Id	When thoughts of him / her pop into my mind

When problems get me down, I find it helps to:

V	Write them down so I can see them clearly
A	Talk or listen to another until my problems sound easier to hear
K	Go for a walk
Id	Mull them over in my mind

When I'm very happy, my world:

V	Takes on a definite and wonderful shine
A	Resonates with total harmony
K	Fits perfectly within the space of my life
Id	Makes sense – I have a knowingness of that

THE SELF-AUDIT

When I concentrate, I most often:

V	Focus on the words or the pictures in front of me
A	Get distracted by extraneous sounds
K	Move around a lot, fiddle with pens and pencils and touch things
Id	Think about the problem and the possible solutions in my head

When I first contact a new person, I usually:

V	Arrange a face to face meeting to know what they look like
A	Talk to him or her on the telephone
K	Suggest we meet in person at an activity or meal
Id	Consider what things we have in common

I remember things best by:

V	Writing notes or keeping printed details so that I can see them
A	Saying them aloud or repeating words and key points in my head with a certain tonality
K	Doing and practicing the activity
Id	Being precise and reciting them over and over

THE SELF-AUDIT

	I think that you can tell if someone is lying if:
V	He or she avoids looking at you
A	His or her voice changes
K	He or she gives you funny vibes
Id	What is stated is illogical or seems manipulative

	I feel especially connected to other people because:
V	How they look
A	What they say to me
K	How they make me feel
Id	They think as I do or have the same world view

	If I am teaching someone something new, I tend to:
V	Use diagrams to help them see
A	Give this person a verbal explanation
K	Demonstrate first, and then let him or her have a turn
Id	Ensure that he/she understands the rationale of this

THE SELF-AUDIT

When preparing for a meeting or exam, I generally:

V	Write lots of revision notes and diagrams
A	Talk over my notes, alone or with other people
K	Get a feeling for the venue
Id	Ensure that the agenda or outcome is precise and unambiguous

I find it easiest to remember:

V	Faces
A	How a person sounds
K	Things I have done
Id	If something makes sense

I tend to say:

V	I see what you mean
A	I hear what you are saying
K	I know how you feel
Id	That makes sense to me

THE SELF-AUDIT

If I was buying something of substantial value, I would:

V Look at pictures and reviews in newspapers and magazines

A Discuss what I need with my friends or colleagues

K Test out many different types

Id Consider price, value for money, service, warranty

When I am learning a new skill, I am most comfortable:

V Watching what the trainer-teacher is doing

A Talking through with the teacher exactly what I'm supposed to do

K Giving it a try myself and work it out as I go

Id When I know that it will be useful in my own life

I first notice how people:

V Look and dress

A Sound and speak

K Stand and move

Id Take time to consider things and other people

THE SELF-AUDIT

STOP HERE
if this self-audit is work-related

CONTINUE ON
if this is a personal self-audit

	In the morning, I especially enjoy awakening to:
V	Either the sun streaming in or an overcast day
A	The sound of nature, like birds singing
K	A warm and toasty comforter or flannel sheets
Id	A planned and logical agenda

	When I listen to a band, I can't help:
V	Watching the band members and other people in the audience
A	Listening to the lyrics and the beats
K	Moving in time with the music
Id	Wondering about the composition's arrangement

THE SELF-AUDIT

I really love:

V	Watching films, looking at art or photography, or people watching
A	Listening to music, or talking to friends
K	Taking part in sporting activities, dancing, eating delicious foods, or drinking fine wines
Id	Spending time alone pondering the mysteries of life

When I engage in my favorite sport, I particularly enjoy:

V	The look of the game, or how I look playing it
A	The sound of the game, such as the thwack of the ball, or the roar of the crowd
K	The feel of the game, such as the grip of the club or the sense of motion
Id	Formulating or guessing at possible outcomes

The subject I enjoyed the most in school came about primarily as a result of:

V	The way it looked on the board or in books
A	The sound of the subject as it was taught to me
K	Getting a feel for it as I learned more about it
Id	Thoughts about how similar it was to a favorite game or activity

THE SELF-AUDIT

I choose household furnishings because I like:

V Their colors and how they look

A The tone of voice as the sales-people describe it

K Their textures & what it feels like to touch them

Id Their practicality and usefulness

At the gym, my satisfaction comes first from:

V Seeing myself in the mirror getting better

A Hearing myself or others say how good I'm looking

K Feeling my body get stronger and sensing it's more in shape

Id Knowing that I am doing it just right

My first memory is of:

V Looking at something

A Hearing something

K Doing something

Id Wondering about something

THE SELF-AUDIT

	On the occasions when I think of a former lover, the very first thing I do is:
V	See the person in my mind's eye
A	Hear his or her voice in my mind
K	Get a certain feeling about the person
Id	Wonder what it would be like if we were still together

	When I meet an old friend:
V	I say "it's great to see you"
A	I say "it's great to hear your voice"
K	I give them a hug or a handshake
Id	I remember the good times

	I find it easier to be with my friends if:
V	They communicate using animation and visual statements
A	They interact with me through easy-to-hear and varying speech
K	I get a feeling that they know where I'm coming from
Id	Our time together is expected to be useful

THE SELF-AUDIT

When I go shopping for clothes, I tend to:

V	Imagine what they would look like on
A	Discuss them with the shop staff
K	Put them on and test them out
Id	Consider quality, price, and durability or wonder what others are thinking of me

When I recall a time when I was immensely drawn to someone, the very best thing that attracted me was:

V	The way this person looked
A	Something he/she said to me, or that you heard
K	The way he/she touched me, something I felt
Id	His / her capacity to think things through

When I love someone, I get an instant experience of:

V	The way we look together - the eyes of love
A	The sound of telling him or her (or being told) ... I love you
K	A feeling or sense of warmth toward that person
Id	Him / her thinking about me

THE SELF-AUDIT

	If I am choosing food off a menu, I tend to:
V	Imagine what the food will look like
A	Discuss the options with my partner
K	Imagine what the food will taste like
Id	Associate the description with my memories of similar food

	During my free time I most enjoy:
V	Reading, observing (nature, TV, scenery, people, etc.)
A	Listening to music and talking to my friends
K	Playing sports / doing crafts or arts projects
Id	Wondering, formulating, remembering, and creating

	At the beach, the first thing that makes me glad to be there is:
V	The look of the sand, the smiling sun, and the ice-blue water
A	The sound of the waves, the laughing wind, and distant whispers
K	The feel of the sand, the salt air on my lips, and the joy of serenity
Id	That this vacation makes sense at a reasonable cost

THE SELF-AUDIT

**Having a conversation at a party,
my whole frame of experience will change if:**

V	The lights get brighter or dimmer
A	The music changes pace
K	The room temperature changes
Id	People interrupt when I am considering things

When I need directions for traveling I usually:

V	Look at a map
A	Ask for spoken directions
K	Follow my nose and maybe use a compass
Id	Research whatever resources are available first

During sex, I like to:

V	Look at what's going on
A	Hear my lover and/or express myself
K	Feel every sensation
Id	Imagine a psychic connection with the other person

THE SELF-AUDIT

When I am choosing a holiday I usually:

V	Peruse the pictures in brochures
A	Listen to recommendations from friends
K	Get a feeling for what it would be like to be there
Id	Research the details of cost, time, or distance

When someone tells me, "I love you" my first experience is:

V	An image of the person loving me, or us together
A	A certain tone of voice saying, "This is wonderful"
K	A feeling of pleasurable contentment
Id	To compare and contrast his/her statement against the actions

When I drive, this is how I navigate:

V	I look for road signs or follow a map of the territory
A	I listen for familiar sounds that point me in the right direction
K	I get a gut feeling or sense of where I am
Id	I prepare precise directions (times, distances, landmarks)

THE SELF-AUDIT

	When I cook a new dish, I like to:
V	Have a picture in my mind as to what it will look like
A	Call a friend for an explanation
K	Follow my instincts, testing as I cook
Id	Consider cost, taste, and nutritional value

	When I recall a particularly wonderful vacation I had, the very first experience I remember is:
V	The way the resort area looked
A	The different way it sounded to me
K	The feeling I got by vacationing there
Id	Discovering that the features and benefits are as booked, paid for, and expected

	Before going to sleep at night, it's important that:
V	The room is nearly dark or pleasantly shaded
A	The room is hushed or muted with pleasing background quiet
K	The bed feels very comfortable
Id	Clear my mind of unresolved conflicts

Finished?

What's Next?

You have probably found that you are a mixture of all profiles. Virtually all of us are.

This result reveals your *primary communication traits*.

> *Men are not prisoners of fate,*
> *but prisoners of their own minds.*
>
> Franklin D. Roosevelt

As with most abilities, these communication skills will quickly improve with practice.

In the days ahead, observe your family, friends, and colleagues. Soon you will notice patterns in the way they communicate.

Begin using these concepts in your everyday communication at work, at home, and at social events. In time, your improved capabilities and skills will become second nature.

Communication Profiles are also Learning Styles

If you have difficulty absorbing new material, you may not be employing your primary communication style.

Understanding this concept and employing it on the job might influence your career advancement.

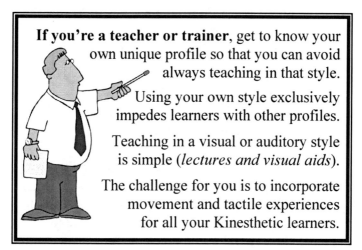

If you're a teacher or trainer, get to know your own unique profile so that you can avoid always teaching in that style.

Using your own style exclusively impedes learners with other profiles.

Teaching in a visual or auditory style is simple (*lectures and visual aids*).

The challenge for you is to incorporate movement and tactile experiences for all your Kinesthetic learners.

Suspected Learning Difficulties

Since our traditional school curricula favor visual and auditory delivery, the kinesthetic learners are often the ones who lose out.

Numerous studies of *kids at risk* have shown that the vast majority of dropouts are kinesthetic learners.

They were unable to sit still and focus for long periods. This behavior either got them into trouble or labeled *hyperactive*.

Sadly, what often followed were prescriptions.

Building Rapport

No matter what your role is in society, good communication with others is crucial, and the skills outlined in this little book can go a long way towards improving person-to-person interaction.

For example, if you are **visual**, and you know that the other person is **kinesthetic**, slow your speech and use the words that kinesthetic communicators use.

- Instead of:
    I see what you're looking for.
- Rephrase to:
    Now I can grasp what you want.

If you are **kinesthetic**, your speech is usually slow and deep. If you answer the phone and the speaker speaks rapidly with a somewhat lively and high-pitched voice, you might reasonably conclude that the caller is a **visual** communicator. If you stay with your slow and deep voice, you are not matching the caller's profile and thus missing an opportunity to build rapport.

If someone with whom you're speaking is slow to respond, then perhaps he or she is experiencing feelings, or preparing and processing an answer so that it will be more meaningful. Be patient.

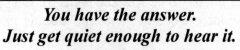

You have the answer.
Just get quiet enough to hear it.

Pat Obuchowski

The Unspoken Signals

During my initial hypnosis training, I found the subject of non-verbal signals particularly fascinating.

People often disregard the use of non-verbal techniques when attempting to establish rapport. For the most part, body language happens at a non-conscious level. This means that whatever non-verbal techniques you use, the other person will likely not be aware that you're employing them.

If you wish to create an atmosphere of trust with someone, an effective two-step approach is to quickly determine his or her primary traits. Then begin using this other person's posture, breathing pattern, and gestures. Unconsciously, this person will sense a vague bond or attachment with you.

Id traits are non-sensory, so we'll focus only on **VAK** and their non-verbal traits.

Visual communicators are neat and orderly, have good posture, breathe high in their chest, gesture upward with their hand, stand back so as to *take it all in*, look up when talking, and stand erect with shoulders straight.

Auditory communicators tilt their head as if on the phone, have rhythmic breathing, drum their fingers or tap their toes, and hold their shoulders back.

Kinesthetic communicators stand close when talking, breathe low and deep in the abdomen, are antsy, touch people to get their attention, look down, gesture downward / point to their heart, touch people when greeting or leaving, dress more for comfort than looks, and slouch.

With Wisdom & Skills Comes Responsibility

One of the precepts of NLP is:
The system with the greatest flexibility has the control.

In other words, in interpersonal dealings, someone who knows how to effectively employ these skills has the opportunity and responsibility to improve the quality of information exchange.

After reading this book, and employing its concepts, **you** will be the one with the skills. You will be the one with the responsibility to adapt to the communication profiles of others.

To really enhance your communication with others, match their particular styles.

You can find out more about this communication model on YouTube and other online resources. My own video is on our website. You can also visit us:

www.YouTube.com/WalshSeminars

Want to communicate better with your family?

Use this self-audit to assess their profiles.
V, A, K, *or* **Id**

Then communicate with words and body language that *each of them* responds to and uses. You may have to interact with each child in a different manner.

Remember that the system (that's YOU) with greater flexibility has more capacity to promote the quality of communication.

Answers for the review quiz on page 12

1. A	11. K	21. A
2. K	12. Id	22. K
3. A	13. A	23. K
4. V or K	14. A	24. K
5. Id	15. Id	25. A
6. A or K	16. K	26. K
7. V	17. K	27. K
8. A	18. V	28. Id
9. K	19. A	29. V
10. A or K	20. V	30. Id

Remember the four promises at the beginning of this book?

Once you understand the different profiles, you can:

→ **Get your point across**
in a way that people will understand

→ **Establish rapport quickly**
to facilitate smother interactions

→ **Absorb information**
with greater ease and comprehension

→ **Enhance your leadership skills**
and accelerate your career

If you have followed the three steps suggested on page 2, then you now have a great foundation to support excellent communication skills.

INTELLIGENCE:
The ability to adapt to changing conditions

Just for a moment, consider intelligence as much more than a score on an IQ test.

Know that intelligence determines and reflects how well we navigate through life's tasks and challenges.

Employees are generally evaluated within the narrow scope of their job descriptions, without consideration of their potential in an enriched environment. Job enlargement and enrichment may offer opportunities for employees to exercise otherwise untapped resources. This is a win-win for the employee and the company.

This book provides an overview of the lesser-known intelligences: *naturalistic, musical, social-interpersonal, spiritual-intrapersonal, bodily-kinesthetic, and spatial.*

Those wanting to strengthen individual intelligences can immediately implement the tangible suggestions contained here.

Born in England and raised near Montreal, **Brian Walsh** was a journalist and broadcaster before joining a major international firm. For much of his thirty-year career he was involved in human resources, specifically staff training.

While living in the Canadian Arctic, Brian served as a Justice of the Peace, and studied Neurolinguistic Programming (NLP) and anthropology. Those experiences and extensive international travel prepared him for working with other cultures. He was then transferred to China where he served as his company's General Manager.

After his return to Canada, he elected early retirement to further his earlier interest in NLP and hypnotherapy. He returned to formal study, and within four years had achieved his PhD.

His dissertation, which focused on accelerated learning techniques, inspired his passion and his bestselling book, *Unleashing Your Brilliance.*

The companion video DVD for his book is *Enriched Learning.*

Brian is dedicated to personal growth and enrichment through his articles, webinars, workshops, and audio / video products.

He has co-authored a self-help book with Jack Canfield and John Gray: *101 Great Ways to Improve Your Life.*

Brian is an NLP Master Practitioner, a Hypnotherapist, an EFT Practitioner, and an Acupuncture Detoxification Specialist.

More Products by Brian Walsh

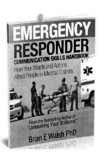

www.WalshSeminars.com

Lightning Source UK Ltd.
Milton Keynes UK
UKOW04f0452230914

239022UK00007B/89/P

Non-Fiction » Self-Improvement » Confidence and self-esteem
Non-Fiction » Career Guides » Education

- ◆ *It's like we're not talking the same language.*
- ◆ *He just doesn't understand me.*
- ◆ *I was very clear in what I said and she still didn't get it.*
- ◆ *Why does he always begin without reading the instructions?*
- ◆ *I really don't understand what my teacher is saying.*
- ◆ *These test questions look so unlike what we were taught in class*
- ◆ *I wrote the instructions down and it's like he simply ignored the*
- ◆ *I know you told me, but I got it all mixed up in my head.*
- ◆ *I perform better when I just do it and not think about it too muc*

Do any of the above sound like you or someone you know?
All of us communicate and learn in our own unique ways.
Understanding your own profile will help you improve your interactic
with colleagues, family, friends, and even complete strangers.

What you'll find in this book can make a dramatic difference in your lif
All you have to do is discover the concepts, do a bit of practice, and th
complete the self-audit.

<u>Enhance your abilities</u>
Once you understand the different profiles, you can
- • *get your point across in a way that people will understand*
- • *establish rapport quickly to facilitate smother interactions*
- • *absorb information with greater ease and comprehension*
- • *enhance your leadership skills and accelerate your career*

Brian Walsh, a specialist in accelerated learning and a
clinical hypnotherapist, has authored and produced
over fifteen books, audios, and videos.

He supports thousands of people in their quest for
personal empowerment by promoting brain-friendly
strategies in his live and online workshops.

WalshSeminars.com

WALSH
seminars

PUBLISHING HOUSE

ISBN 978-0-9866655-5-4
90000

9 780986 665554

IMPERMANENCE

SAM R GERAGHTY